D1709832

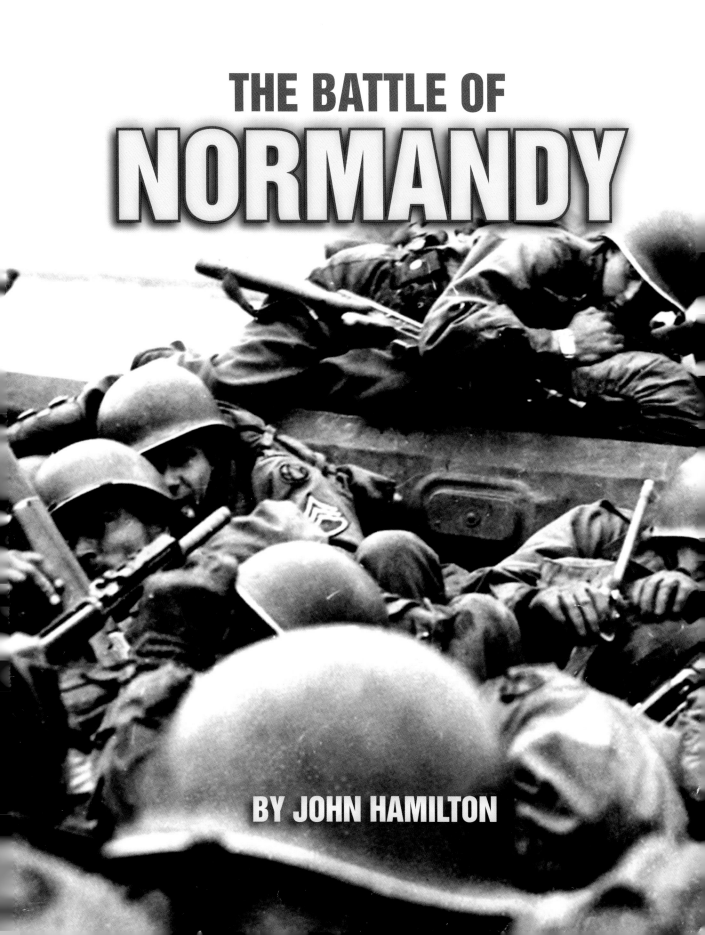

THE BATTLE OF
NORMANDY

BY JOHN HAMILTON

VISIT US AT
WWW.ABDOPUBLISHING.COM

Published by ABDO Publishing Company, PO Box 398166, Minneapolis, MN 55439. Copyright ©2014 by Abdo Consulting Group, Inc. International copyrights reserved in all countries. No part of this book may be reproduced in any form without written permission from the publisher. ABDO & Daughters™ is a trademark and logo of ABDO Publishing Company.

Printed in the United States of America, North Mankato, Minnesota.
102013
012014

 PRINTED ON RECYCLED PAPER

Editor: Sue Hamilton
Graphic Design: John Hamilton
Cover Design: Neil Klinepier
Cover Photo: Getty Images
Interior Photos and Illustrations: AP Images, p. 9 (Eisenhower), 9 (Bradley), 11 (Rommel), 14, 18, 22; Corbis, p. 5, 6, 8 (Roosevelt and Churchill), 10, 16, 26, 29; Digital Stock, p. 15, 21; Getty Images, p. 13 (flamethrower and Spitfire), 19, 20, 24, 27, 28; Granger, p. 11; John Hamilton, p. 4, 17; National Archives and Records Administration (NARA), p. 1, 9 (Montgomery), 12, 13, 25.

ABDO Booklinks
To learn more about Great Battles, visit ABDO Publishing Company online. Web sites about Great Battles are featured on our Book Links pages. These links are routinely monitored and updated to provide the most current information available. Web site: www.abdopublishing.com

Library of Congress Control Number: 2013946976

Cataloging-in-Publication Data

Hamilton, John, 1959-
   Battle of Normandy / John Hamilton.
   p. cm. -- (Great battles)
Includes index.
ISBN 978-1-62403-206-6
1. World War, 1939-1945--Campaigns--France--Normandy--Juvenile literature.   I. Title.
940.54--dc23

2013946976

CONTENTS

PRELUDE TO
INVASION

World War II (1939-1945) was the deadliest conflict in human history. By mid-1942, after nearly three years of bloody warfare, the Axis alliance of Germany, Japan, and Italy seemed unstoppable. German blitzkrieg attacks had swallowed up most of Europe. In the Pacific, the Japanese empire continued to expand. On December 7, 1941, Japan attacked the United States naval base at Pearl Harbor, Hawaii. The United States finally declared war and threw its manpower and industrial might into the struggle.

In the following two and a half years, the Allies, including the United States, Great Britain, and the Soviet Union, won major victories. Despite these successes, Allied leaders knew that in order to defeat Germany, they had to keep fighting and free all of Western Europe. The next step would be the invasion of Normandy, France.

By mid-1942, Nazi Germany and its allies had defeated and occupied most of Europe and North Africa.

4

*U.S. soldiers in a Higgins boat
approach the French coast of
Normandy on D-Day, June 6, 1944.*

OPERATION
OVERLORD

The Allied plan to attack Adolf Hitler's German army in Western Europe took years to plan. As early as 1942, Soviet Union leader Joseph Stalin demanded that the Allies, especially the United States and United Kingdom, attack from the west. Stalin's own forces were struggling for survival against the Germans on the Eastern Front.

The Allies decided to launch an amphibious attack from southern England across the English Channel. The invasion was code named Operation Overlord.

Although German army commanders expected an attack from across the English Channel, they didn't know exactly when and where the invasion might occur. The Allies used fake radio messages and other trickery to keep the Germans guessing, and to force the enemy to spread its army thin over a wide area. The Allies even created a phony "phantom" army in southeastern England to make the Germans think the attack would take place over the narrowest stretch of the English Channel. However, the real invasion would be directed where the Germans didn't expect it: the French region of Normandy.

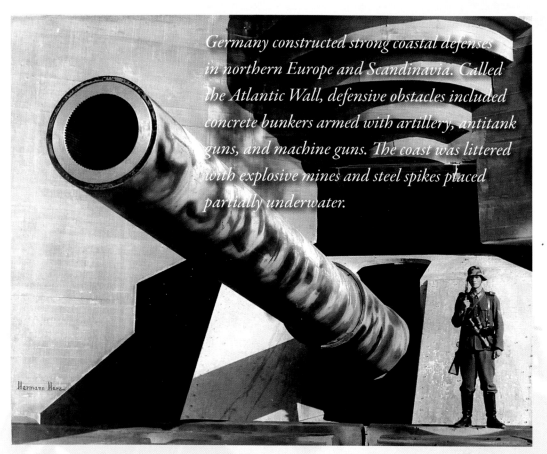

Germany constructed strong coastal defenses in northern Europe and Scandinavia. Called the Atlantic Wall, defensive obstacles included concrete bunkers armed with artillery, antitank guns, and machine guns. The coast was littered with explosive mines and steel spikes placed partially underwater.

The Allies spent many months training soldiers for the amphibious assault. Sometimes the training was deadly. In April 1944, nearly 1,000 American soldiers and sailors died because of training accidents and skirmishes with the German navy.

Finally, by June 1944, the Allies were ready. Stormy seas churned the waters of the English Channel. The Allies took advantage of a break in the weather and designated June 6, 1944, as D-Day, the first day of the invasion. In the early morning hours, a vast flotilla of more than 5,000 ships carrying 175,000 soldiers, 50,000 vehicles and other equipment crossed the English Channel toward Normandy. More than 11,000 fighters and bombers flew overhead to support the invasion. Operation Overlord was well underway. It would be the largest invasion in history.

LEADERS OF THE ALLIES

The two countries most responsible for planning and carrying out the Normandy invasion were the United States and the United Kingdom. The president of the United States was **Franklin Delano Roosevelt** (1882-1945). He was the country's 32nd president, serving from 1933 to 1945. He was a strong leader who guided America through tough times, including the Great Depression. Although he was confined to a wheelchair (he contracted polio in 1921), Roosevelt had an optimistic personality, and knew how to best manage government resources.

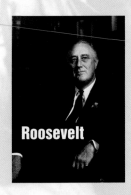

Roosevelt

He let his generals make important military decisions, but his policies improved the industrial might of the United States, which greatly helped the Allied war effort.

Sir Winston Churchill (1874-1965) was the prime minister of the United Kingdom for most of World War II, from 1940-1945 (and again from 1951-1955). He was a shrewd politician. He warned people in the 1930s of Nazi Germany's desire to conquer Europe. During the war's darkest days, Churchill's brilliant speeches rallied the British people.

Churchill

Eisenhower

American five-star **General Dwight D. Eisenhower** (1890-1969) was the Supreme Commander of Allied forces in Europe. He was perfect for the job: diplomatic but tough. He brought together a diverse group of armies from several countries and coordinated the D-Day attack on Normandy. Eisenhower's nickname was "Ike." After the war, the American people elected him as the 34th president of the United States.

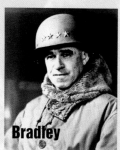
Bradley

American **General Omar Bradley** (1893-1981) was a brilliant field commander who worked closely with General Eisenhower. Bradley commanded the U.S. First Army during the Normandy invasion. He was popular with American troops. Because of his reputation, he was often called "the soldier's general." Bradley eventually rose to the rank of five-star general.

British **General Bernard Montgomery** (1887-1976) commanded the Allied 21st Army Group during the Normandy invasion. Often too cautious in his battle planning, Montgomery was nevertheless admired by the soldiers under his command. Nicknamed "Monty," he later earned the title of field marshal, the highest rank in the British Army.

Montgomery

LEADERS OF THE
AXIS

Hitler

Axis leaders included Germany's Adolf Hitler (1889-1945), Italy's Benito Mussolini (1883-1945), and Japan's Emperor Hirohito (1901-1989) and General Hideki Tojo (1884-1948). World War II began in 1939, after Germany invaded Poland. Japan conquered most of China and other countries in East Asia. Germany signed agreements with Italy and Japan called the Axis alliance. Hitler and Mussolini's armed forces quickly overwhelmed almost all of Europe and North Africa. Hitler's dream was to create a powerful German empire he called the Third Reich, a dictatorship he alone would rule.

Adolf Hitler led Germany from 1933 until 1945. He was head of a political group called the National Socialist German Workers' Party, better known as the Nazi Party. In Germany he was called the Führer (leader). He was a brilliant politician, a riveting speechmaker, and a brutal dictator. He ordered the Holocaust, the mass murder of six million Jews, along with hundreds of thousands of other people. He did not manage the war very well, and never fully trusted his generals or advisors.

Rommel

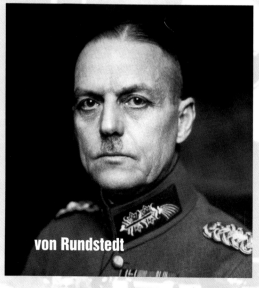

von Rundstedt

Field Marshal Erwin Rommel (1891-1944) was a famed German tank commander. He was known as the "Desert Fox" for his daring battlefield skills in North Africa. In 1944, Adolf Hitler placed Rommel in charge of improving the Atlantic Wall. Rommel boosted his troops' morale and oversaw the placing of mines and underwater obstacles. Severely injured in an air attack on July 17, 1944, Rommel was hospitalized during the final part of the Normandy invasion. Later that year, accused of being involved in a plot to assassinate Hitler, Rommel was forced to commit suicide on October 14, 1944.

Field Marshal Gerd von Rundstedt (1875-1953) was one of the most important planners of the German army. Early in the war, he commanded forces that invaded both Poland and the Soviet Union. During the first hours of the Normandy invasion on June 6, 1944, von Rundstedt asked for tank reinforcements to be sent to the coast. His request was denied by Hitler. The Führer changed his mind later that day, but the order came too late. The Allied invasion force already had a firm foothold on the beaches of northern France. Later that year, the ailing von Rundstedt was dismissed by Hitler.

TACTICS AND WEAPONS

The Allied plan on D-Day was to launch an all-out combined arms attack on the Normandy coast. This part of the invasion was called Operation Neptune. The complicated plan included many steps. Just before dawn, airborne troops would be dropped inland to disrupt Nazi forces and capture bridges and other key targets. Long-range artillery on Allied naval ships would weaken German shore defenses. Thousands of troops, supported by aircraft, tanks, and other vehicles, would land on the beaches and fight their way inland, establishing a solid Allied foothold in German-occupied France.

During World War II, factories invented new ways of riveting and welding that produced mass quantities of reliable, deadly

Naval artillery, such as these massive 16-inch (41-cm) guns firing from a U.S. battleship, supported Allied troops on D-Day.

firearms and explosives. Automatic weapons, often called machine guns, weren't as accurate as rifles, but their increased firepower could be devastating. A single soldier armed with a machine gun could wipe out an entire enemy squad at close range. Other weapons used by soldiers on both sides included hand grenades, flamethrowers, and anti-tank weapons such as bazookas. Air power, including fighters and bombers, was used to devastate enemy troops, vehicles, and supply routes.

American Browning M2 heavy machine gun

German Flamethrower 35

British Supermarine Spitfire

A squad of American soldiers, armed with rifles, uses a Sherman tank as cover while on patrol.

AIRBORNE ASSAULT

As the main fleet of Allied ships crossed the English Channel on D-Day, about 17,000 airborne troops were dropped inland from the beaches of Normandy. Their pre-dawn mission was to protect the flanks, the east and west sides, of the invading Allied soldiers. At that time, it was the largest airborne assault in history.

The first wave of troops numbered more than 13,000. Approximately 925 C-47 transport planes flew them from their bases in southern England to Normandy. Once over the French countryside, they bailed out of their planes and parachuted to the dark ground below, landing five hours before the main Allied attack. They were later joined by 4,000 reinforcements, plus additional weapons and heavy equipment, aboard more than 300 silent British Horsa and American WACO CG-4A plywood gliders that landed on French soil.

Paratroopers from the British 6th Airborne Division and the 1st Canadian Parachute Battalion were dropped into the invasion zone's left flank (the eastern sector). Soldiers from the U.S. 82nd and 101st ("Screaming Eagles") Airborne Divisions landed in the west, on Normandy's Cotentin Peninsula.

U.S. paratroopers prepare to jump over Normandy on D-Day.

Supreme Allied Commander U.S. Army General Dwight D. Eisenhower encourages paratroopers of the U.S. 101st Airborne Division—the "Screaming Eagles"—a day before the D-Day invasion. Paratroopers, many carried by silent glider aircraft, landed in France the night before the main invasion. They succeeded in capturing critical bridges and roads despite heavy losses.

Confusion, harsh weather, and German anti-air defenses caused many troops to land miles away from their landing zones. Hundreds of paratroopers were cut down by German fire even before they could untangle themselves from their parachutes. Many paratroopers, weighed down by heavy loads of gear, landed in marshes and drowned. Dozens of gliders crashed, killing all on board. In total, about 8,200 airborne troops were killed, wounded, or reported missing during the Normandy air assault.

Even though they were badly scattered, the brave and resourceful soldiers managed to regroup. They fought fiercely in the dark, capturing or blowing up bridges and German communications centers. Although many goals were not finished by dawn, the airborne troops caused much confusion among German leaders. An effective German counterattack was never launched. If not for the airborne assault, the main Allied invasion force might have been stopped at the beaches of Normandy.

HITTING THE
BEACHES

The Allies divided the Normandy invasion zone into five sections, which were spread out along 50 miles (80 km) of coastline. From west to east, the zones were code named Utah Beach, Omaha Beach, Gold Beach, Juno Beach, and Sword Beach. American forces were responsible for attacking Utah and Omaha Beaches in the west. British forces attacked Gold and Sword Beaches,

American soldiers in a Higgins boat prepare to land at Normandy.

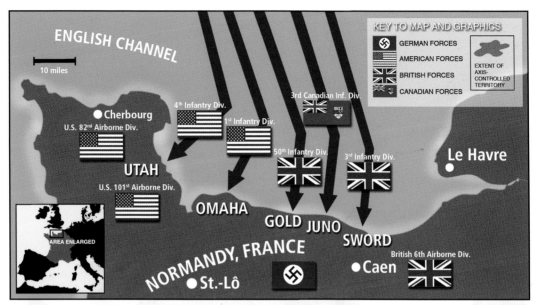

On June 6, 1944, American, British, and Canadian forces stormed the coast of Normandy, in northern France. The beaches were divided into five sections: Utah, Omaha, Gold, Juno, and Sword. American and British airborne troops also took part in the invasion against well-defended German forces.

while Canadian soldiers landed at Juno Beach.

Just before the troops arrived, the Allies launched a heavy aerial and naval bombardment against German coastal defenses. Bombers and fighters flew overhead and dropped thousands of tons of explosives on enemy bunkers. Just offshore, six battleships and 19 cruisers unleashed massive firepower with long-range guns. The German soldiers who suffered

through this barrage were shocked and disoriented by the attack.

Next, the Allies sent in waves of infantry to storm the beaches. They timed the attack to occur during low tide, when German underwater obstacles would be exposed and could be avoided. After crossing the English Channel in massive transport ships, the troops boarded small landing craft called Higgins boats, which could each hold 36 soldiers plus a crew of three.

Officially called Landing Craft, Vehicle, Personnel (LCVP), the Higgins boats were made mostly of plywood. They were designed by Andrew Higgins, who owned Higgins Industries of Louisiana, to transport people and equipment through swamps and marshes. Early in World War II, the military recognized how important they could be in amphibious assaults, and ordered them in large numbers. Each 36-foot (11-m) -long boat could carry soldiers and equipment to shore relatively quickly, at about 14 miles per hour (23 kph).

Once a Higgins boat reached the beach, its entire front ramp dropped down, allowing the soldiers to rush into combat. Thousands of Higgins boats were used during the D-Day invasion. After D-Day, Supreme Allied Commander Dwight Eisenhower said, "Andrew Higgins... is the man who won the war for us. ... If Higgins had not designed and built those LCVPs, we never could have landed over an open beach. The whole strategy of the war would have been different."

The first troops, weighed down by their packs and weapons, reached

American troops advance toward German positions during a D-Day reenactment.

Normandy at about 6:30 a.m. They were met by a murderous combination of enemy machine gun fire, artillery barrages, mines, and in some cases, death by drowning.

Allied tanks assisted the troops. Some were transported in large landing craft. In many cases, Sherman M4 tanks "swam" to the beaches under their own power. These amphibious tanks used propellers and inflatable rafts to keep them afloat. Unfortunately, many tanks were swamped by heavy seas and sank to the bottom of the English Channel.

After several hours of furious combat, Allied troops on four of the five beaches were firmly in control. German casualties were high. Their defenses collapsed after the pummeling by Allied air and sea artillery, followed by the surprise amphibious attack by commandos and infantry. Allied forces began to link up, regroup, and move farther inland, firmly establishing a foothold in northern France.

BLOODY OMAHA
BEACH

While the D-Day attacks on Utah, Sword, Gold, and Juno Beaches were proceeding well, it was a different story at Omaha Beach. The United States 1st and 29th Infantry Divisions endured the worst weather conditions along the entire invasion front. During the 10-mile (16-km) journey from the mother ships to shore, many landing craft were swamped by waves. The men who made it to the beaches were seasick and wobbly on their feet. Rough seas and high winds drove many landing craft far away from their targets. Maps became useless.

Heavy clouds and poor aim by Allied aircraft and naval artillery failed to dent the German defenses. Many radios required by artillery spotters were lost when landing craft were sunk or destroyed.

The first wave of troops to land on Omaha Beach faced what seemed like certain death. Many men were cut down the moment they stepped foot on the sand.

On D-Day, many Allied troops made their final assault in Higgins boats.
In this photo, the boat's ramp has dropped down, allowing American infantry
to wade ashore at Omaha Beach—directly into heavy enemy fire.

American soldiers help survivors ashore after their landing craft was hit and sunk by German coastal defenses.

Sometimes, German 88mm artillery shells scored direct hits on the Higgins boats, completely destroying the landing craft and killing all on board.

The beach was a mess of obstacles. There were concrete blocks and slanted poles with explosive mines strapped to their ends. Seaward-pointing steel rails ripped open the hulls of the landing crafts. A tangled web of barbed wire made movement almost impossible in some places.

A line of tall cliffs ran parallel to the landing zone. Up to 150 feet (46 m) high, they gave the German defenders a perfect view of the beach. From a network of concrete bunkers and machine gun nests, the Germans rained death on the Allied troops below.

The toll on the Americans was terrible. Some groups suffered casualties of 90 percent or more. Those who survived the first onslaught were forced to huddle behind sand dunes or burning vehicles as German machine guns and mortars continued to pound the beach. Many wounded soldiers, unable to move, drowned as the tide began to rise. Medical corpsmen frantically worked under fire to save as many men as they could.

As the day wore on, the Americans realized that the only way to survive was to move forward, toward the cliffs. Colonel George Taylor rallied his men. "Two kinds of people are staying on this beach," he said. "The dead and those who are going to die. Now, let's get... out of here!"

The Americans regrouped and began mounting effective attacks against the Germans. Heavy smoke from grass fires and exploded vehicles and ammunition gave them cover as they inched their way off the beach. Army Rangers fought their way up gaps between the bluffs. They fought furiously to destroy the enemy's concrete bunkers and other strongpoints. Allied destroyers sailed close to shore, risking enemy fire, and began pounding German positions. All the while, more and more landing craft brought waves of fresh troops and weapons to the invasion zone.

By sunset on D-Day, 34,000 troops were ashore at Omaha Beach. The U.S. 1st and 29th Divisions suffered about 2,000 men killed, wounded, or missing. Despite these high losses, the invasion was a success. The Allies had a firm foothold in France.

Failure at Omaha Beach could have affected the outcome of the entire war. Without linking up all five invasion zones, a German counterattack could have driven a wedge between Allied forces. With their units splintered and weakened, the Allies might have fought to a draw, or even been forced to retreat back to England.

Unfortunately for the Germans, the American men at Omaha Beach were brave and resourceful. They fought against overwhelming odds. Much blood was spilled, but their sacrifice ensured that the tide of World War II had turned.

THE NORMANDY
BREAKOUT

By the end of D-Day, June 6, 1944, Allied forces had gained a firm foothold in France. More than 100,000 troops had landed. Millions would follow in the weeks to come.

After shattering German defenses, the Allies towed artificial harbors, called Mulberries, across the English Channel. The harbors made possible the rapid offloading of reinforcements and supplies.

American soldiers take cover in a ditch near the French town of Ste.-Saveur-le-Vicomte.

Within days, the Allies were pushing far inland. German defenders fought stubbornly. The Germans used the region's sunken roads and tall hedgerows to hide nests of machine gunners and antitank weapons. The Allies fought for every inch of new ground. Bad weather made things even worse.

After six weeks of bitter fighting, the Allies finally began forcing the Germans back. British and American airplanes had almost total control of the French skies, destroying German counterattacks and supply routes.

No longer confined by the tangled Normandy countryside, Allied troops, supported by tanks and aircraft, swept through France. Paris was liberated by August 25. The American Third Army, commanded by General George Patton, pushed the enemy back toward Germany. After years of planning, at the cost of thousands of lives, the Battle of Normandy was over. The Nazis in Western Europe were on the run.

Allied ships unload troops and a massive amount of equipment at Omaha Beach on June 7, 1944.

WHY DID GERMANY LOSE THE BATTLE?

The Allied invasion of Normandy was successful for many reasons. From the beginning, the Germans believed the attack would come in the Calais area, which was the shortest route across the English Channel. By attacking in Normandy, the Allies caught the Germans by surprise. Also, most of the German defenders in Normandy were poorly trained. Many of them surrendered or deserted as the Allies broke free from the beaches.

Allied commanders were unified in how they carried out their battle plans. The German generals, on the other hand, disagreed about how to fight the Allies. German leader Adolf Hitler interfered with local commanders' decisions. From his bunker in Berlin, he controlled the German defenses, even though he didn't know about local conditions.

Field Marshal Rommel, seen here supervising German coastal defenses, grew frustrated with Adolf Hitler's decisions.

About 210,000 German soldiers were taken prisoner during the Battle of Normandy.

German Field Marshals von Rundstedt and Rommel asked for more freedom to act, but Hitler refused. Late on D-Day, the Führer finally agreed to send in extra tanks, but by then it was too late.

After the breakout of Allied forces deep into Normandy, Hitler's decision making again proved disastrous. Instead of withdrawing his forces and regrouping, the Führer ordered his men to stand their ground and stop the Allies from advancing. After weeks of bitter fighting, the Germans had no choice but to retreat toward their home border and exit France. The Allies enjoyed almost total control of the skies. Their warplanes continually harassed German ground forces. Allied air superiority, plus a massive supply of fresh soldiers and equipment, proved too much for the battered Nazi army.

THE BATTLE'S AFTERMATH

The invasion of Normandy was the most decisive battle of World War II in Western Europe. Allied success sealed the fate of Germany's ambitions to occupy the continent. It was now fighting a war with two fronts: one against the Soviet Union in the east, and the other against Allied forces in the west. Hitler's Third Reich was doomed to failure. It lost access to the raw materials, sea ports, and factories of Western Europe. Under relentless attack from all sides, it was only a matter of time before the Nazi regime collapsed. By May 1945, less than one year after D-Day, Germany surrendered.

The Normandy invasion was a great success, but it took its toll in blood. More than 425,000 Allied and German soldiers were killed, wounded, or reported missing. Tens of thousands of civilians also died.

Today, the Normandy American Cemetery and Memorial is located on a bluff overlooking Omaha Beach. It contains the graves of 9,387 American soldiers, most of whom died on D-Day or during the Normandy invasion. On the Walls of the Missing are inscribed another 1,557 names. The cemetery, and 26 others like it with war dead from both sides, are a solemn yet grim reminder of war's ultimate cost.

An American soldier shares a laugh with a French woman.

Army veteran Arnold Franco pays tribute to fallen comrades at the U.S. cemetery in Normandy, France.

GLOSSARY

ALLIES

The Allies were the many nations that were allied, or joined, in the fight against Germany, Italy, and Japan in World War II. The most powerful nations among the Allies included the United States, Great Britain, the Soviet Union, France, China, and Canada.

AUTOMATIC WEAPON

A type of firearm that uses the force of the explosion of a shell to eject the empty cartridge case, put the next shell in position, and then fire it. This sequence continues as long as the trigger is pressed. A semi-automatic weapon fires once each time the trigger is pulled.

AXIS

The Axis powers were the World War II alliance of Germany, Italy, and Japan.

BATTLE OF NORMANDY

The name for the fighting that took place between D-Day, June 6, 1944, and the end of August, 1944.

BLITZKRIEG

A German word meaning "lightning warfare." It described a new strategy that the German military used in World War II. *Blitzkrieg* called for very large invasions to overwhelm the enemy quickly with combined land and air attacks in order to avoid long, drawn-out battles.

CASUALTY

Soldiers and civilians reported as either killed, wounded, or missing in action.

D-DAY

A code name that stands for the day a military operation begins. It has been used in many different battles, but today it usually refers to the beginning of the Battle of Normandy, June 6, 1944.

HIGGINS BOAT

A landing craft (boat), designed by American Andrew Higgins, used in amphibious assaults. Higgins boats transported troops from larger ships to the beaches during an attack. A Higgins boat could carry about 36 soldiers to shore. After a ramp was lowered onto the beach, the soldiers exited the boat through the bow.

NAZI

The Nazi Party was the political party in Germany that supported Adolf Hitler. After 1934 it was the only political party allowed in Germany. This is when Hitler ruled Germany with total power.

OPERATION NEPTUNE

The beach-landing assault phase of Operation Overlord. It began on D-Day, June 6, 1944, and ended June 30, 1944.

OPERATION OVERLORD

Code name for the Allied invasion of northwest Europe. It began on D-Day, June 6, 1944, and ended when the Allies crossed the River Seine on August 19, 1944.

INDEX